Essential Teachings of Yoga

~ Pathways to Awaken the Bliss of Being ~

A commentary on the

Upadesha Sāram

of

Shri Ramana Mahārshi

श्री

उपदेश सारः॥

By Shri Rāmānanda Mayī

Blooming Lotus Press

Published by Blooming Lotus Press

ISBN 978-0-9918521-0-9

Set in Fanwood/Linden Hill/GentiumAlt fonts

Printed in Bali, Indonesia

Caring for Dharma Books

Dharma books contain the sacred teachings of the sages and have the power to show the way towards liberation. As such they should be treated with respect and reverence. Please never place them directly on the floor, step over them, point your feet towards them or take them into bathrooms. They should be kept in a clean place and ideally be covered in fabric when transported. No other mundane objects should be placed on top of them. If it is necessary to one day dispose of them it is best to give them away to a library, or immerse them in a lake, river, or ocean, rather than throwing them in the trash. Thank you for your understanding, love and care of this book.

om namaḥ shivāya gurave
sat chit ānanda mūrtayai
nishprapañchāya shāntaya
nirālambāya tejase
om shantiḥ shantiḥ shantiḥi

ॐ

We Invoke the Pure Consciousness of the Inner Teacher
Who Appears as the Bliss of Self Awareness
Who is the Eternal Peace Beyond Appearances and
Who Illuminates the Path to Freedom
May There Be Only Peace

Humbly offered to the lotus feet of
the silent sage of Aruṇāchala,
Shri Ramaṇa Mahārshi,
whose compassionate eyes bestow
the light of wisdom
and by whose blessings these words were written.

Bhagavan Shri Ramana Maharshi

Notes on the English Translation

In an attempt to introduce this brilliant text to a wider, non-sanskrit knowing audience, the translation of the verses from Sanskrit into English has been done in a loose and free flowing manner. In keeping with the original spirit of the Sanskrit text the author has made every attempt to clearly articulate the *Mahārshi's* message into modern English and has taken the liberty of adjusting the wording to suit the essence of each verse, rather than translate it directly. Many great translations of *Upadesha Sāram* are available that strictly adhere to the common translation of Sanskrit words into English. However, the author has found that these scholarly translations are excellent resources for those already familiar with Indian philosophy but not easily read or understood by the average western student of yoga. As such, a more easily readable version has manifested and the author hopes it will be widely accepted, while forgiveness for any mistakes in its translation is asked.

Notes on the Sanskrit Verses

The Sanskrit verses that adorn the beginning of each verse are all reproductions of Shri Ramana Mahārshi's own original hand-writing.

Notes on Transliteration

The conversion of Sanskrit words into English found in this book is very similar to the guidelines of the "International Alphabet of Sanskrit Transliteration." The reader should be aware that for ease of reading and chanting for those not familiar with Sanskrit sounds two important exceptions have been made:

ch = c and sh = ś

Likewise, due to the use of the Fanwood Text font used throughout the book the three letters "ṃ" "ṇ" and "ṣ" do not display correctly and have been omitted and replaced by the letters "m" "n" and "s" respectively.

For the ease of the reader hyphens have been placed in between long words where the correct number of syllables is available.

Due to these and other minor phonetic changes the following transliteration scheme has been adopted to match the IAST guidelines for some of the words found in this book:

Krishna = kṛṣṇa	*hridayam* = hṛidayam	Mahārshi = Mahāṛṣi
nishkāmya = niṣkāmya	prāna = prāṇa	prānāyāma = prāṇāyāma
Ramana = Ramaṇa	samskāra = saṃskāra	shri = śrī
yogis = yogiḥ	yogas = yogaḥ	upanishads = upaniṣad

Contents

Introduction

Upadesha Sāram is perhaps the most luminous gem in the treasure house of yogic texts. Written in the year 1927, by the great sage of South India, Bhagavan Shri Ramana Mahārshi, it is a relatively new addition to the corpus of yogic literature. Yet its newness should not undermine its authority, as it succinctly condenses the entirety of thousands of years of yogic wisdom and extracts the essential teachings of *yoga* in a humble 30 verses.

It systematically expounds both the theory and practices of all four branches of the sacred tree of classical yoga. Offering not only theoretical insight into *Karma Yoga,* the path of selfless service, *Bhakti Yoga,* the path of self-surrender, *Rāja Yoga,* the path of self-discipline and *Jñāna Yoga,* the path of self-awareness, it also has the capacity to dispel all confusion in the mind of the seeker as to which path is most appropriate for them. The other revered classical yogic text, the *Bhagavad Gītā,* too, expounds these four paths of yoga as the means to liberation. Although some may say that the message of the *Gītā* is indirect, whereas the Maharshi's exposition on these four paths is crystal clear, leaving no room for any doubt to arise.

The Upadesha Sāram definitively asserts that the Natural State of Unified Consciousness, called *yoga,* is only One. All the various techniques and methods, grouped into these four categories: *Karma, Bhakti, Rāja* and *Jñāna,* exist only to meet the unique temperaments and levels of spiritual maturity of each individual. Ultimately they all cultivate and merge into the same one Essence.

Upadesha means teaching or instruction, while *Sāram* invokes essence or that which is essential. As such, what is contained herein is the Essence of Spiritual Instructions or 'Teachings on the Essence'. *Ramana Mahārshi,* with the greatest elegance, takes only the essential, inner core of each path of *yoga* and condenses it into a seed-like form, which comprises each verse. Once reflected upon deeply, these verses sprout within one's own mind and reveal their nectar-like inner meaning, satiating one with the bliss of wisdom.

Upadesha also has another meaning; to show that something is very near. So long as the misconception that we are not Spirit itself is held, we may feel that It is far away from where we are here and now. In these essential teachings on *yoga* the Mahārshi reveals that Spirit is so close and intimately near that it is actually the inner most Self of all.

May this realization dawn upon us all, so that we may all live in the Bliss & Peace of Self-Awareness.

Om Shantiḥ, Shantiḥ, Shantiḥi

Part 1

Karma Yoga

~ The Path of Selfless Service ~

1

कर्तु राज्ञया
प्राप्य तेफलम् ॥
कर्म किंपरं
कर्म तज्जडम् ॥१॥

kartur-ājñāyā prāpyate phalam
karma kiṃ paraṃ karma taj-jaḍam

Through the inherent order of Nature actions give results. Is Karma then Absolute? No, it is constantly changing and lacks Consciousness.

The *Mahārshi* commences these essential spiritual instructions by first drawing our attention to the ever elusive operating principle that governs the entire cosmos – *karma,* the law of cause and effect. As with all great spiritual traditions originating in the East, the primary cause of our sense of seperation and dissatisfaction in life is identified to be *āvidya,* or ignorance of our natural state of freedom. Also called *māyā,* or illusion, this innate ignorance is synonymous with *karma* – the state of continual activity.

Everything appears to be interconnected and because of this natural order, causes give birth to effects. It is due to the completeness and interdependence of each and every object in creation that innumerable causes lead to specific effects. Take as an example a mango tree. Within this simple object the entirety of the cosmos is interwoven. It is composed of innumerable atoms and contains an elemental constitution brought together and made cohesive through the gravitational force of our solar system and beyond. In its sap are drops of water that once flowed through all the rivers, lakes and oceans of the Earth. The leaves of the tree, have photosynthesized sunlight and given birth to its flowers. This same mango tree provides us with the oxygen necessary to sustain our life force, while we give back carbon dioxide to sustain its life. In the mango seed all these numerous forces lay dormant - ready to produce another single tree when the conditions are right. Everything is interconnected; nothing stands in isolation from the whole. This inherent natural order of the universe is governed by *karma* and by its very operation, entire galaxies spin and the tiniest of atoms vibrate.

Is *karma* then Absolute? Is it the Supreme Principle upon which all depends? The *Mahārshi*'s answer to these questions is both simple and eloquent. Because causes produce effects, which later become the causes for further effects ad infinitum, *karma* is forever in a state of flux and impermanence; hence, it cannot be the unchanging Absolute. For anything to be Real or True, it by definition, cannot exist in one moment and cease to be in another. The Absolute must be eternal and changeless. As such, *karma* is only a Relative phenomenon whose operating principles are limited to the realm of time and space.

Karma is merely a mechanism, a universal principle that in and of itself, is not conscious or Self-aware. It blindly functions without the capacity of changing its own trajectory, much in the same way that an arrow which has been shot from a bow must follow its pre-ordained course.

Here the *Mahārshi* points out three very important foundational points:

1. It is due to the interdependent and interconnected nature of the Whole, not the individual elements within it, that things occur as they do.
2. The things that do occur are temporary and not permanent.
3. The doing of actions, though seemingly impelled by the individual, is in fact occurring through a supra-egoic force. Yet, even this force (karma) is in and of itself, unconscious.

In this one simple verse and its three essential points, the entirety of *karma* has been succinctly expounded and thus the road paved for the revelation of how to release oneself from the illusionary sense of seperation that the path of *yoga* seeks to illuminate.

2

कृतिम होदध्यौ
पतन कारणम्॥
फलम शाश्वतं
गतिनि रोध्यकम्॥२॥

kṛti-mahodadhau patina-kāraṇam
phalam-ashāshvataṃ gati-nirodhakam

Activity is obstructive to liberation, as any results obtained are impermanent, thus creating more bondage.

The Absolute, Unified State of Consciousness called *Yoga* is defined as simply a natural state of "Being", free from the impulsion to do anything to gain fulfillment. *Karma*, or the path of "Doing", on the other hand is not only contrary to *yoga* but is its antagonistic and obstructive counterpart.

Each living being seeks happiness and wishes to avoid suffering; this is a self-evident truth. We are all are motivated to act in ways that we believe will lead us to the permanent and eternal happiness we seek. We strive for an ideal job, seek the perfect relationship, want a nice home, look forward to enjoyable food, and chase after money to secure the outer comforts of life. We each take countless courses of action each day to help us obtain that which we have been conditioned to believe will give us enduring happiness. But yet who has truly found lasting happiness?

Through this reflection upon our own direct experiences the fundamental human dilemma presents itself. Each one of us has an ongoing search, knowingly or not, for eternal happiness yet continually discover that it evades our efforts. We have been conditioned since birth to believe that happiness lies outside of ourselves, and that if only things could be different in our external world, we would gain the permanent satisfaction that we seek. As such, we are constantly engaged in activities trying to fill ourselves from the outside, when actually true happiness has never been found there by ourselves nor others.

Karma Yoga is that branch of yogic wisdom that addresses this very issue and offers us a suitable remedy. Before proposing a plausible solution to this age-old dilemma, the *Mahārshi* points out in this verse that as long as one believes that doing anything will give full liberation, be it mundane action or even so-called spiritual activities, they will inevitably be disappointed. Any movement of body, speech or mind, will have innumerable causes as its base and thus lead to corresponding effects. These effects in turn become causes for further effects, with this cycle continuing on and on. This cyclical pattern is called the wheel of *karma* and within it all living beings are unconsciously impelled to act out the effects of previous causes. This is similar to the scenario of a caged mouse that is caught spinning around in a wheel while chasing after an elusive piece of cheese. With each step the mouse takes, his little feet land on the wheel which he has previously made to spin since his first step. Retracing his steps over and over again, the little mouse is unaware that each footstep he takes in the present is impelled by a footstep of the past.

So long as we keep revolving around this wheel of karma, engaging in fruitless activity that leads us away from our natural state of Being, we will be continually evading the peace and happiness that lies within.

3

ईश्व रार्पितं
नेच्छ याकृतम्॥
चित्त शोधकं
मुक्ति साधकम्॥३॥

īshvarāpitaṃ nechayā kṛtam
chitta-shdhakaṃ mukti-sādhakam

Actions done while remembering the One and without a desire for their intended results, purify the mind and are a means towards liberation.

The law of cause and effect is so intricately interwoven that it is impossible to know the exact outcome of all the actions that we put into motion. Sometimes we act in ways whereby our foresight is strong and things turn out the way we envision and desire them to be. While at other times because of innumerable unseen forces, the outcome of our intentions is much different than what we expect. As such, we are elated when we get what we want and sorrowful when we get what we don't want. This mental/emotional state of attachment to pleasurable outcomes and aversion to undesirable outcomes gets reinforced over time creating our individual characters with their unique conditioning of likes and dislikes. Each one of us is attempting to get more of what we want and less of what we don't. Thus in both subtle and obvious ways, humans try to continually impose their will upon

Nature, trying to manipulate her delicate balance. This type of control, whereby one attempts to increase their share of pleasure and decrease displeasure, is the habitual reactive conditioning of the human mind. Upon a superficial investigation this may seem normal and natural, for who doesn't want pleasure and want to avoid pain? Yet it is only after a sincere inquiry and much life experience that the wise realize that pleasures do not give lasting happiness. The continual, obsessive desire to chase after pleasure actually takes away from being able to experience the full enjoyment that life offers. In this compulsive desire to have more and more, so few actually fully enjoy what they have in each moment. This continual grasping for pleasurable outcomes is termed *kama,* or desire.

Desire is the central hub upon which the wheel of *karma* turns. For each desire fulfilled or obstructed, a new desire for more pleasure or less pain puts new chains of cause and effect into motion. The inevitable outcomes of fulfillment or denial of what we desire is common to us all, and in the end, we often come out wanting more or wishing things could be different. So long as we continue to seek pleasure and avoid pain, we will be living a life filled with dissatisfaction and regret.

Yoga is unique in its presentation of happiness for it posits that true, enduring happiness is within our grasp because it is our natural state. This enduring happiness, or *ānanda,* is inherent within us but can only be realized once we cease to desire anything more or less than what we are experiencing in each and every moment. This complete acceptance of what Is, without grasping for something else, is the Natural State of Being called *yoga.* By shifting our attention to the present moment, embracing what is, and letting go of all expectations and attachments, we soon come to find that all we are searching for is with us; right here, right now.

To realize this state of deep acceptance the *Mahārshi* prescribes a remedy to the chronic state of dissatisfaction upon which the mind spins. Instead of obsessively attempting to control the flow of Nature's results, he graciously offers us a path of soft surrender and yielding to what Is. Precisely because controlling the effects of innumerable interconnected and interdependent causes is impossible, the *Mahārshi* recommends that we let go of the expectations we hold and surrender the results of our actions into the universal flow of Nature. We simply accept that the Whole, not the egoic individual, is doing everything, and claim no ownership of the outcomes of the actions performed by the body/mind.

When we let go of desiring for a specific outcome from our actions and accept whatever happens, be it positive or negative with an even and balanced mind, we effectively break the chains of *karma*. When we let go of mentally holding on to the fruits of our actions, we are able to loosen the grip of attachment and aversion which eliminates the arising of new internal causes to shape further effects. This cessation of reactivity purifies the mind and allows it return to it its natural state which is pure and full of virtues like humility, patience, forgiveness, generosity, wisdom and compassion.

To surrender into Nature's flow does not mean that we stop all action, for that is impossible, as physical action is inevitable. What it means is that we stop being bound by our mental conditioning and live freely, without being effected by the ups and downs of life. We are impelled to act, and act we must, however we are not impelled to grasp on to the outcomes of our actions.

Instead, *Karma Yoga* recommends that we engage in desire-less actions, called *nishkāmya karma*, and offer the results of all that we do for the welfare of the Whole; rather than the gratification of our individual selves. This subtle shift of attitude is the essence of *karma yoga* and leads one on a path where selfless service, or *seva*, to the One begins. Attuning all thoughts, words and deeds to Spirit and acting without desiring anything, purifies the mind of the egoic feeling of separation, until the ego eventually dissolves completely. Ultimately, the individual merges back into its source – the One Absolute Consciousness, which is pure Bliss.

Part 2

Bhakti Yoga

~ The Path of Self Surrender ~

4

काय वाङ्मनः
कार्य मुत्तमम् ॥
पूज नंजप
श्चिन्त नंक्रमात् ॥४॥

kaya-vān-manaḥ kāryam-uttamam
pūjanaṃ japash-chintanaṃ kramāt

The actions done through body, speech and mind, such as rituals, chanting and meditation, are increasingly superior in this ascending order.

Having established the nature of *karma,* and the methods of escaping its grasp through the performance of selfless and desire-less actions, the *Mahārshi* now turns his gaze towards *Bhakti Yoga* – the path of devotion and surrender. *Karma Yoga* seamlessly evolves and weaves itself into the path and practices of devotion as its essential core is an attitudinal shift towards what is encapsulated by the proverb "May thy will, not mine, be done."

No longer seeking to impose one's self-centered will upon creation, naturally the sense of a higher power emerges. Those who sincerely experiment with the practices of *Karma Yoga* immediately begin to feel a greater sense of ease in their lives as huge reservoirs of mental/emotional tension, anxiety, and stress are freed from the subconscious controlling mechanisms which dictate all self-motivated actions. Along with this, is experienced an incredible awe and wonder of how spontaneously and effortlessly all their needs and wants are taken care of by a benevolent and compassionate presence that begins to guide their lives. A deep gratitude and thankfulness often develops and the *karma yogi* naturally wishes to express their love and affection towards this liberating force.

For those who feel a strong impulse to express their gratitude and love the *Mahārshi* points out that ritualistic ceremonies, chanting the names of Spirit and meditation are all excellent means to channel devotion towards the One. However, these methods also become more impactful and powerful in this very same progressive order. Ritualistic actions are done with the body and vary among spiritual traditions. They are the types of activities found in ceremonial functions within temples, churches, mosques, sacred natural spaces and personal home altars. Usually a form of the Divine is chosen to represent one's personal or communal ideal of the Formless Spirit and is invoked and worshiped in various ritualistic ways. Often incense, candles, flowers, food offerings and holy water accompanies the rituals with the aim of invoking the Presence of Spirit through ceremonial worship.

Chanting is a subtler means than ritual to invoke the presence of the One, as it is involves using sacred sound vibrations to recall the presence of the Absolute. Each sacred tradition has its own songs, hymns, chants or *mantras* that can be used to focus and concentrate the mind, as well as purify our speech. Utilizing the power of sound to alter awareness is common to all cultures and societies. *Mantras*, or luminous sacred sounds, especially have the capacity to turn our awareness inwards and invoke the silent presence of pure consciousness.

The most effective method however, is pure silence itself, which is discovered through deep meditation. Silence is the true language of Spirit that transcends all boundaries. All rituals and chanting ultimately culminate in silence.

5

जगत ईशधी
युक्त सेवनम्॥
अष्ट मूर्त्तिभृ
द्देव पूजनम्॥५॥

jagata īsha-dhī-yukta-sevanam
aṣṭa-mūrti-bhṛd-deva-pūjanam

Selfless service done, while holding the view that the world is itself Spirit, is the true worship of the One in all its forms.

The highest form of ritual worship is to act with the view that all is Spirit. Actions done in this way are naturally compassionate and self-less. The *Mahārshi* offers us a most sublime vision of the actual nature of the world. He suggests that in the state of unified consciousness, where all is perceived as One and not many, this very world is experienced as That completeness. This very world, with all its suffering, joy, pleasure and pain is itself the phenomenal expression of Spirit. In other words the world is Spirit manifest; the Formless One having taken the form of all experience. To then deny the world is to deny Spirit itself.

The *Mahārshi* advises us not to run away from the world, but rather to embrace it with wisdom. He suggests that we view all living and non-living beings as manifestations of Spirit and that we should serve Spirit selflessly by alleviating the sorrow we see around us in any way that is appropriate. At times this may mean serving humanity through social services, such as feeding the poor, offering health care or education. And at other times, sitting and meditating quietly while emanating waves of peace and harmony from the depth of one's Heart, is a huge benefit to all beings. All these examples are excellent forms of *seva*, or selfless service.

Once perfected, this practice of seeing the world as Spirit manifest transforms one's perception of the entire creation into a heavenly realm where each moment is an opportunity to witness the miracle of existence. We can look into the very eyes of God in each living being whose lives we may touch and offer our gratitude for being alive and having the opportunity to show compassion.

"When you see it is someone's *karma* to suffer, consider it your *dharma* to alleviate their suffering" said another wise sage. Although it may be one's *karma* to experience their life as it is, it is in the nature of Spirit to continually give and relieve suffering. To be the instrument of the One and witness the expression of unconditional love through the body/mind becomes the greatest joy of all. When all actions become purified through love and compassion then the whole world becomes one's altar.

6

उत्त मस्तवा
दुच्च मन्दतः॥
च्चित्त जंजप
ध्यान मुत्तमम्॥६॥

uttama-stavād-ucha-mandataḥ
chittajaṃ japa-dhyānam-uttamam

Better than singing songs in praise of Spirit, is the repetition of sacred sounds, either aloud, by whisper or mentally.

Elaborating further on the *Bhakti Yoga* practices of singing and chanting, the *Mahārshi* states that the repetition of sacred sounds, either out loud, by whispering, or by repeating it internally, is more impactful than chanting or singing spiritual hymns or chants. As powerful as gospel, *kirtan, bhajan,* indigenous chanting, trance music, qu'ali or any other method of using sound to alter awareness can be, the repetition of sacred sounds is considered even more powerful according to the *Mahārshi*. Sound inherently has the capacity to externalize or internalize our awareness. Certain sounds, such as phones ringing, voices arguing, and alarm bells, obviously pull our attention outwards. While other sounds, such as water flowing, birds chirping and the luminous sacred sounds called *mantras,* draw our awareness inwards.

Mantras can be used in a number of ways to bring awareness into its natural state. The easiest method of utilizing *mantra,* is to repeatedly chant them out loud. This can calm and introvert the mind. Chanting a *mantra* so softly that it is barely audible with only the lips moving is the next stage of drawing the awareness inwards. Softly chanting *mantras* creates a very rhythmic and balanced brain wave pattern that then prepares the mind for purely internal mental repetition, which is the final stage towards the withdrawal of the senses.

Continual mental repetition of sacred sounds ultimately drowns out all other thoughts so that awareness rests only upon one singular thought. This is called *dhyāna* or meditation, single-pointed attention upon one object – in the case of *Bhakti Yoga* it is usually a *mantra.* Sustained practice ultimately allows the subject to merge into the object of meditation, so that the chanter, the chant and the process of single-pointedly chanting are experienced as one complete whole.

To merge and unite with one's beloved form of Spirit is the ideal of *Bhakti Yoga.* This requires great devotion, surrender and an uncompromising faith that this union is possible. Often the form of the Beloved is associated with a name, and it is this holy name that is invoked through *mantra.* Some also prefer to visualize the form of their beloved in between the eyebrows or in the center of the chest while chanting their *mantra* to induce greater concentration. The important point however, is that the mental repetition and/or visualization leads the mind inwards to its natural state of silence.

7

आज्य धारया
स्रोत सासमम् ॥
सरल चिन्तनं ।
विरल तःपरम् ॥७॥

ājya-dhārayā srotasā samam
sarala-chintanaṃ viralataḥ param

Unbroken attention, which flows smoothly like the water of a river, is superior to focus which waivers.

When speaking of devotional meditative practices, like the repetition of mantra or *japa*, the *Mahārshi* here confirms that single-pointed attention towards the object of devotion is more powerful when it is continual and unbroken. For the mind to merge into the object of its love, intense and complete attention must be devoted to this singular yearning.

By nature the mind is constantly changing, as it grasps to experience everything other than its own natural state of silence. Forever ensnared by attraction and aversion, the mind seeks to experience happiness and love through the external world. In *Bhakti Yoga* practice, we take the mental & emotional states that we experience, transmute their energy, and direct it towards our ideal form of Spirit. Be it Divine Light, a God or Goddess, a prophet, saint, sacred text, spiritual teacher, or natural phenomenon like a holy mountain or sacred river, all of one's focus must remain without wavering upon a form or object which reflects the presence of Spirit. Buddha said that "whatever the mind dwells upon, that it becomes," and in *Bhakti Yoga* when the mind is attuned to an object that reflects unconditional love it begins to take on this same quality. Through continuous focus on its Beloved's form the entire personality of the devotee transforms and begins to emanate the same love, compassion, kindness, forgiveness, humility, patience and virtues of their chosen form.

Normally it is the emotional body that has the strongest conditioning of attachments. While thoughts of the mind change quickly the moods of the emotional body last for longer periods of time and color the type of thoughts we experience. *Bhakti Yoga* practices work directly with the emotional body and particularly with its capacity for relationship. *Bhakti Yoga* is primarily about developing a personal relationship with your Beloved by channeling the emotional states of the mind towards its embrace. *Bhakti yogis* often are impelled to relate to Spirit in some personal, yet transcendental way, through a love story with Divinity. They may commune with Spirit as father, mother, lover, friend, or even as their child.

Through dance, songs, chants and calling out the name of their Beloved, their minds in time become imbued with the same characteristics as their ideal. As these inner virtues develop, so too does the mind grow in calmness and stillness. Eventually the heart of the devotee is so enraptured with their beloved form that they can even have visions of the invisible presence they worship, in a visible and even physical form. Such is the power of the mind to attract that which it focuses upon intensely.

By repeated and unbroken devotion, the mind eventually loses itself in its object of intense longing. Eventually it merges into the Formless Spirit, which is the substratum of all forms. This state of unbroken unity with the Beloved is the ideal and consummation of *Bhakti Yoga.*

8

भेद भावना
त्सोऽह मित्यसौ।
भाव नाऽभिदा
पाव नीमता॥८॥

bheda-bhāvanāt-soham-ityasau

bhāvanā bheda pāvanī matā

Meditating with the attitude that "I am Spirit" is more purifying than meditation that posits a separation between the individual and the Supreme.

The initial stages of *Bhakti Yoga,* the feeling of love and devotion towards Divinity well up in the heart of the devotee but is often accompanied by a strong feeling of separation. Due to the past conditioning of the dualistic mind, whose nature is to perceive distinctions and the parts rather than the whole, even when thoughts and emotions turn towards spirituality the lingering traces of dualism superimpose themselves on the quest to unite with the One. This confusion leads the devotee to mistakenly believe that there is a separation between themselves and Spirit, and hence, a need to re-unite with their beloved.

In truth no such division actually exists. The highest teaching of *yoga, tantra* and *vedānta* all clearly state that Spirit is One, incapable of ever being separate or dual. All beings exist within Spirit, as Spirit. Yet spiritual awareness need not exist within them. Hence the aim of all yoga is not to re-unite or bring together that which is separate; as no such separation ever has been, is now, nor can ever be possible. The aim of *yoga* is merely to remove the ignorance that obscures this truth, through the direct experience of Unity.

To aid the process of removing this ignorance of the natural state of Unity, the *Mahārshi* advises that when one meditates upon Spirit it is better to do so with the feeling that "I am One with Spirit," or "Spirit am I," or if one prefers, "I am God." Rather than admitting the false belief that Spirit is outside of us, or in some far away heavenly realm, or inherently different than our present condition, it is more appropriate to admit the truth of what Is.

Taking the attitude that "I am Spirit," or "*So Ham,*" is a higher expression of *Bhakti Yoga,* as the devotee directly reconditions the dualistic mind by dwelling upon a thought-form that more accurately reflects Reality. Upon sustained practice the individuality of the personal ego begins to dissolve into the inherent Oneness of Reality. At this stage prayer, love and devotional acts are all directed inwards and one's own divinity begins to reveal itself.

9

भाव शून्यस
द्भाव सुस्थितिः॥
भाव नाबला
द्भक्ति रुत्तमा॥९॥

bhāva-shūnya-sad-bhāva-susthitiḥ
bhāvanā-balād-bhaktir-uttamā

By the strength of this type of meditation, one becomes established in the state of True Being, devoid of all thoughts, which is the Supreme Devotion.

How can the vision of the Absolute Consciousness be realized if one continually assumes and affirms that they are separate from it? *Yoga* essentially means "unity," while all its various practices are better described as means towards "union." So long as one holds the mistaken view that one is separate from Spirit the methods to remove this ignorance will remain necessary. But once the actual direct experience of the Unified Supreme Consciousness is tasted this false concept falls away, as do all the practices that presume otherwise. By the sustained application of the one-pointed affirmation that "I am Spirit," the mind dissolves into a singular concept that is closer to Truth. In due course the layers of the impure mind with all its dualistic ideas begins to peel way; much like the skin of an onion. Layer after layer of conditioning, egoic misconceptions and ignorant ideas about one's self, others, the world and Reality are all peeled away.

Ultimately as the final thought "I am Spirit" is held for prolonged periods of time without any other discursive thoughts, the mind comes into a place of utter stillness. Free of all conditioned thoughts or ideas about one's Self, the unconditioned natural state of Pure Being dawns within the Heart. The profound experience of purely allowing yourself to exist, as you are, is the state of *Yoga*. This is the highest form of devotion; for it is here that you realize your oneness with everything and unite with the Beloved.

All prayers cease, all mantras end, all devotional acts culminate and all longing to unite with the Beloved exhaust themselves in the blissful silence of the natural state of *Yoga*. Even the idea that "I am Spirit" must be dropped for this experience to reveal itself. It is one of the final obstacles, which once removed, reveals that the essence of the mind is actually empty, yet paradoxically full of the whole of Existence at the same time. This emptiness is the nature of the pure mind - free of thought, ideas, and concepts and conditioning, which can at once also grasp the entirety of Existence. Capable of both resting in pure silence and simultaneously perceiving the layers of thoughts, emotions and actions, the True Self, or Supreme Consciousness, is eternally witnessing its own Existence, without attachment or aversion. This is the deepest acceptance and surrender into That which Is - it is the Supreme Devotion.

10

हृत्स्थले मनः
स्वस्थता क्रिया ॥
भक्ति योगबो
धाश्च निश्चितम् ॥१०॥

hṛt-sthale manaḥ svasthatā kriyā
bhakti-yoga-bodhāsh-cha nishchitam

Resting the mind in its natural state within the sacred space of the Heart is the essence of karma, bhakti, rāja and jñāna yoga.

Having established the theory and practices of both *Karma* and *Bhakti Yoga,* here the *Mahārshi* pauses and gives the quintessential teaching of this entire scripture. Before introducing the lofty paths of *Rāja* and *Jñāna Yoga* he states that no matter what practices, techniques, or forms one may adopt on their spiritual path, their essential aim and ultimate culmination ends when the mind finally abides in its natural resting place – the Heart. After a tiresome journey through dense forests of thoughts, deserts of doubts, valleys of fear, and oceans of emotional waves, at long last the mind ceases its struggle and returns home to rest. Whatever vehicle one uses to cross this vast terrain of ignorance is of no real import, as all these methods are only to establish the mind in the Heart, where it can experience permanent peace and happiness.

The message that there are countless paths to the One Truth, is at the very core of *yoga.* The sages, since time immemorial have stated, "Truth is One, yet the paths are many." The beauty and universality of yoga theory and practice is eloquently summed up in this simple statement. The path of *yoga* is a universal and all-embracing means of spiritual development and evolution. Beyond the dogma of religions, traditions or other limiting belief systems, and irrespective of time, place or culture, the essential teachings of *yoga* exist - veiled behind a mask of various names and forms. From caring for the poor and needy, to Christian gospel prayers and Catholic Hail Mary's, Buddhist chanting and sacred art, Islamic prayer times and prostrations, Jewish holy days and rituals, Hindu temple worship and sacred fires, Native sweat lodges, Animistic offerings, Rastafarian consecrations, New Age sharing circles to Ecological campaigns to heal Mother Earth all these various means are simply means to bring the mind into the Heart through devotion and self-surrender. Though many amongst us may not yet be aware of this goal, the *Mahārshi* makes it explicit in this very verse.

Even the advanced means of *Rāja* and *Jñāna Yoga* have the same aim in view. Because this essential point has not been fully grasped spiritual seekers around the world continue to debate, while materialistic minds continue to doubt and question the existence of Spirit because they falsely see different goals. One wants *Nirvana,* the other Heaven. One wants to re-unite with their ancestors, another to have a love affair with *Krishna.* One yearns to see the Light, another to become *Buddha.* Yet all the while, those whose minds rest in the Heart know only Oneness. All paths lead to the Truth that there is only One Supreme Consciousness that permeates all. *"Tat Tvam Asi,"* You Are That, proclaim the yogis. Let go of the illusion of separation, by surrendering into the Heart and simply Be As You Are.

Part 3

Rāja Yoga

~ The Path of Self Discipline ~

11

वायु रोधना
ल्लीय तेमनः॥
जाल पक्षिव
द्रोध साधनम्॥११॥

vāyu-rodhan-al-līyate manaḥ
jāla-pakṣivad-rodha-sādhanam

By restraining the breath the mind becomes still like a bird caught in a net. This is an efficient method to control the mind.

Introducing the topic of *Rāja Yoga*, the *Mahārshi* penetrates deeply into the core of all the multifarious practices and identifies the essential discipline of *rāja yogis* – control of the breath. To establish the turbulent mind in its natural state of pure awareness, the *rāja yogis* take the breath to be the vehicle which helps them cross the ocean of suffering and leads them to the peaceful shores of tranquility.

Rāja Yoga is a large umbrella term under which many other specialized paths of self-discipline fall. Other spiritual disciplines such as *kriyā yoga, nāda yoga, mantra yoga,* and *haṭha yoga* all essentially can be labeled as forms of *Rāja Yoga* (as can certain spiritually based forms of martial art, such as Tai Chi or Chi Qong). All of these methods share as their primary theme, self-discipline and control of the breath in one form or another.

Rāja means a king, and taken allegorically within the context of yoga, a *rāja yogi* is one who is the master of his or her kingdom – the body and mind. The path of self-mastery is thus *Rāja Yoga,* in which its adherents have preserved countless, often secret, techniques to still the mind through the breath, and awaken its full potential.

This verse seamlessly weaves together the highest practice of *Bhakti Yoga,* meditation on the Beloved, with the essential practice of the *rāja yogi*, meditation on the breath. Both paths require single-pointed attention on an object. For the *bhakti yogi* it is a name and form of their highest ideal, whereas for the *rāja yogi* it is the breath.

The mind and breath have a very intimate connection, and recently modern research has confirmed through scientific studies, what yogis have known for millennia. The mental and emotional processes we experience daily deeply affect our breathing patterns. When we are angry we breathe fast and shallow, when in grief our breath is staggered and broken, when we are calm our breath is slow and steady, and when we release tension we often sigh. *Yogis* have known this for countless generations and have an entire subtle science of breath called *swara vidyā* which explains these correlations. What *yoga* adds to these "new" scientific discoveries, however, is that the states of mind affect not only the breath, but also the health of the body. Numerous health conditions can be traced to irregular breathing patterns. As well, excessive stress, tension and negative thinking adversely affect the organs, immune system and our longevity. In terms of practical application however, what is even more important is that this process also works in reverse. That is, if we systematically alter the body and breath, the mind in turn, will respond in predictable ways. This is the essence of the science of *Rāja Yoga*.

Ramana Maharshi likens the mind to that of a bird which flies from one thought to another and is very difficult to catch. However, through the consistent practice of breath awareness, slowly this wild bird is caught in the net of mindfulness. If the breath is observed, suspended, or regulated, the mental processes correspondingly slow down and eventually become still enough to observe a singular object. This process is called meditation, or *dhyāna*.

12

चित्त वायव
श्चित्क्रि यायुताः॥
शाखयो र्द्वयी
शक्ति मूलका॥१२॥

chitta-vāyavash-chit-kriyā-yutāḥ
shākhayor-dvayī Shakti-mūlakā

The mind which has the function of knowing, and the vital air which has the function of doing, are like two branches of the One Cosmic Energy which is the Source.

This verse expands on the previous verse, explaining that both the breath & the mind have a common root, and thus explains how they correlate to each other. This root is called *Shakti*, or cosmic energy, in the *yoga*, *tantra* and *vedānta* texts. *Shakti*, deified as the Divine feminine force, is the very source and substance of creation. Through Her inherent intelligence She sculpts the entire cosmos, from the greatest galaxies down to a speck of dust, using Herself as the material base. *Shakti* is the power of Consciousness to manifest itself as the entire universe, and on a personal level, as each individual body/mind.

When *Shakti* condenses into an individual She becomes known as *kundalinī*. A portion of this *kundalinī* energy permeates the entire body/mind while a greater potential reservoir is localized in the human nervous system at the base of the spine where it lies dormant. *Rāja yogis* seek to awaken this dormant aspect of *kundalinī* by utilizing various techniques aimed at influencing its dynamic aspect, which they call *prāna*. Once awakened, the *kundalinī* unveils its previously dormant state to reveal itself as the Supreme Consciousness.

The dynamic aspect of *Shakti* in the individual expresses itself as both the mind, endowed with the faculty of thinking, cognizing and knowing, as well as the vital air, or *prāna*, which gives energy to the body to act. As long as one of these aspects is in motion, so too will be its counterpart. That is, when the *prāna* is in motion, the mind is busy with thoughts, whereas when the mind is quiet, the prana becomes still.

If the mind is experiencing positive thoughts and emotions, the *prāna* is likely to flow with few obstructions in a generally upwards direction. While if there are selfish or more negative thoughts, the *prāna* is obstructed in the subtle energy body and has a tendency to move downwards. *Rāja yogis* seek to raise the vibration of *prāna* in the body/mind by introducing a greater volume of it into the subtle nervous system; a system made up of *chakras*, or energy centers, and the *nadi* energy currents.

Prāna is readily available in all the 5 elements. Initially *rāja yogis* will strictly control their diet and choose foods, which are the earth element, with the highest vibrations like fruits and special herbs. They also utilize the water element by drinking pure water with high vibrations, often sanctified by prayer. They learn how to harness the fire element by the power of the sunlight, to charge themselves with vital life force. However, for the air element, they primarily use special breathing techniques to infuse their body/mind with large reservoirs of prana. Once the *prāna* levels are increased and regulated, the mind feels an abundance of positive thoughts and emotions and ultimately becomes very calm and stable.

With increased clarity and stillness of mind, *rāja yogis* then access the greatest storehouse of *prāna* – the space or ether element - by directly absorbing prana from the cosmos through meditation. When the *prāna* is in such high abundance and vibrating at a very high frequency, it can flow through the subtle body efficiently and clear away any blockages of energy. With a free flow of movement through the subtle network of *nadis*, the *prāna* then accumulates in the *chakras* and becomes very still. The dormant *kundalinī* then awakens, as this accumulated inflow of energy amasses in the *sushmnā*, the central energy channel within the spine, and reveals the Pure Light of Consciousness.

13

लयवि नाशने
उभय रोधने ॥
लयग तंपुन
र्भवति नोमृतम् ॥१३॥

laya-vināshane ubhaya-rodhane
layagataṃ punar-bhavati no mṛtam

Restraint of mind is of two types; dissolution by which the mind subsides temporarily but later resumes functioning, and dissolution by which complete stillness is attained without the mind ever reemerging.

Rāja Yoga emphasizes the control of *prāna* as a means to restrain the mind. It does not initially engage the mind directly but instead uses the breath, the physical vehicle of *prāna,* to indirectly influence the mind. Many *Rāja Yoga* techniques have some form of breath control, called *prānāyāma,* as their support. Through these various breathing techniques the breath slows down to such a great extent that it may appear that *yogis* are not even breathing. When the inhale and exhale become so minute, rhythmic, and subtle, the mind too becomes very still. At this point, when the mind is completely focused and absorbed in the breath, it merges with it. This is called *dhyāna,* or the intense one-pointed focus of meditation. Once mastered, the mind temporarily dissolves into pure silence and dwells there until conceptualization resumes and the breath is altered.

In the state of *dhyāna*, the conscious mind temporarily ceases processing both external stimulus, like sights, sounds, tastes, smells and sensations, as well as internal stimulus like memories, desires, day dreams, hopes, fears and other mental and emotional states. This suspended state of deep inner focus may appear from the outside to be very passive but from within the inner world of the *yogi* it is intensely active. A tremendous self-effort is necessary to enter and maintain this one-pointed focus which simultaneously is opening and purifying the subtle energy body. Correspondingly, the brain-wave patterns of the *yogi* are triggered to cycle though the alpha, theta and delta frequencies, which correspond to the hypnogogic, dreaming and deep sleep states. This allows the *yogi* to consciously access the subconscious and unconscious portions of the brain and peacefully witness and release deeply ingrained conditioning patterns, called *saṁskāras*.

Meditation is like a waking sleep. As the brain wave patterns alter, meditators can relax so deeply that they can easily lapse into unconscious sleep or dreamlike fantasy if their minds are not alert through these transitions. But unlike the relaxation of dream and deep sleep, meditation requires that full conscious awareness penetrates into these subconscious and unconscious states. By simply witnessing the deep recesses of the mind, without attachment or aversion to all that is encountered, the mind lets go of all conditioning. Anger, fear, greed, jealousy, lust, pride and other negative emotional patterns are accessed at their root and through calm mindfulness, the habit of self-identifying with them dissolve.

The practice of mindfulness or witnessing one's thoughts, is a powerful catalyst for self-transformation that completely alters the personality and psyche of the individual, allowing space for the natural virtues of generosity, humility, trust, devotion, joy and compassion to express themselves. Meditation is like cleaning the dirty house of our mind. First we must remove the most visible mental and emotional garbage, like anger and fear, and then we can brush away other self-limiting patterns. Through watching our breath and witnessing the mind, we eventually dust the cupboards of false views, and empty the closets of attachment and aversion. Ultimately even the inner chambers of our mind, which hides the deepest ignorance, are purified.

With each plunge into the deep ocean of meditation, the waves of the mind are made even more pure, calm and still. In due course we reach a point when the inner waters become so completely still that all self-identification with the egoic structure ceases. This complete stillness of mind is called *samadhi*, or equal vision, where one experiences and abides in Reality as it Is. This is the ultimate aim of all forms of *Rāja Yoga*.

14

प्राण बन्धना
ल्लीन मानसम् ॥
एक चिन्तना
न्नाश मेत्यदः॥१४॥

prāṇa-bandhanāl-līna-mānasam
eka-chintanān-nāsham-etyadaḥ

The mind, having subsided by restraining the breath, becomes permanently still by intensely focusing on a singular thought.

This verse describes the means by which *dhyāna*, or meditation, consummates into *samadhi*, or the state of Unified Consciousness. When the stillness of mind has been induced through breath control, it is but a fleeting and temporary state. As soon as the breath unconsciously alters, the calmness of the mind is disturbed. As such *prānāyāma*, or breath control, is not effective enough to bring about *samadhi* – though it can easily propel one into deep meditation. To take the next step, the *rāja yogi* must now confront the mind directly. Thankfully however, due to *prānāyāma*, the task of stilling and stabilizing the mind has been made significantly simpler.

Instead of having to wade through the muck of discursive thoughts and restless emotions, *prānāyāma* makes the mind like a clear and wave-less ocean. At this stage, by single pointedly focusing the mind like a lazer beam upon only one object, one can cut through the illusion of seperation and have the full vision of Unity. It is for this reason that some form of breath control is often recommended by so many spiritual practices. It is much more difficult to gain insight into an agitated mind, as opposed to a mind that has been sedated and made calm through *prāṇāyāma*.

The initial vision of Reality that most *yogis* experience is called *savikalpa samadhi*. In this state an unexplainable bliss enraptures every atom of your being and you feel as expansive as the entire cosmos. You feel at One with everything and everyone as if everything exists within you as yourself, yet without the feeling of individuality. The 2 hemispheres of the brain meld into one another and the central energy channel in the spine is suffused in vibrant white light as each atom of your being pulsates with bliss. The fontanel at the top of the skull seems to physically open and rays of Divine Light shower the entire field of perception with a brilliant radiance. It is utterly intoxicating and fills one with the deepest ecstasy, love and wisdom.

Lying hidden within this experience however, are the subconscious seeds of conceptualization which temporarily lay dormant to allow this sublime state to unfold. As soon as any seed of idea, thought, memory or mental and emotional phenomenon sprout, the *yogi* is hurled back down into the limited consciousness of the body/mind. It is usually only after repeated experiences of *savikalpa samadhi* that the seeds of conditioning are all exhausted and the yogi attains the state of *nirvikalpa Samadhi,* in which all individuality is effaced once and for all so that all that remains is the Supreme Reality in its pristine state of non-dual Consciousness.

15

नष्ट मानसो
त्कृष्ट योगिनः ॥
कृत्य मस्ति किं
स्वस्थि तिंयतः॥१५॥

naṣṭa-mānasotkṛṣṭa-yoginaḥ
kṛtyam-asti kiṃ svasthitiṃ yataḥ

There is nothing left to do for the yogi who has conquered the mind and is established forever in the Natural State of Being.

For the foremost yogi who has tasted the pure Bliss of Self-Awareness through *nirvikapla Samadhi,* what remains to be done? Having made the supreme effort of allowing the mind stream to be absorbed into the ocean of Absolute Consciousness, a true *yogi* has nothing left to do. There is not even an individual left to do it!

The goal has been attained and upon reaching one's destination all that is left to do is to rest in the joy of being aware of one's unlimited existence. All actions of the mind cease upon its final dissolution into eternity. The body however, continues to act, impelled by the natural forces of physical *karma.* This however is only an appearance, as from the viewpoint of the *yogi* the body has no real independent existence nor an operator to make it act. It is a mysterious and paradoxical riddle that only the enlightened amongst us have insight into. Sages report that upon the experience of enlightenment even though they appear to continue to think, feel and act in only the most noble and altruistic ways, their experience is only of complete stillness. All actions happen spontaneously with no personal will operating their apparent actions in the world. Only Spirit exists – the Supreme doer behind all actions; unknowable through the mind, and yet the Natural State of Being.

Part 4

Jñāna Yoga

~ The Path of Self Awareness ~

16

दृश्य वारितं
चित्त मात्मनः॥
चित्त्व दर्शनं
तत्त्व दर्शनम्॥१६॥

dṛshya-vāritaṃ chittam-ātmanaḥ
chittva-darshanaṃ tattva-darshanam

Setting aside the fascination with both the objective and subjective phenomenon, when the mind looks within to find itself all that is seen is Consciousness – the One Reality.

Having expounded on the philosophy and practices of *Rāja Yoga*, the *Mahārshi*, midway in his teachings, turns his compassionate gaze towards *Jñāna Yoga* to which the remainder of this text is dedicated. *Jñāna Yoga*, or the path of wisdom, is profound, yet elusive in its simplicity. Its central theme in both teachings and practical application is the cultivation of Self-Awareness. Though it is true that its practice only bears fruit for the most mature and lucid of truth seekers, it is often misunderstood as a path only for the intellectual or scholarly type. In actuality, learning and accumulated conceptual knowledge are the greatest obstacles on this path which emphasizes deep and Heart felt intuitive apprehension of Reality.

Though *jñāna yogis* can study scriptures, memorize verses, become proficient in scholastic debates or become well versed in philosophy, all of this is unnecessary and a true *jñāna yogi* will claim to know nothing at all - save the True Self which is their essence. On this path of deep contemplation upon the nature of Reality, the rational mind actually obstructs the truth of simply what Is when it attempts to grasp the nature of Reality. This is due to its dualistic nature, which is inherently contrary to the nature of the True Self, which is non-dual – as it is the One Reality. Accustomed to perpetually relying on a conceptual reference point in order to relate to the world, the mind cannot comprehend the basic truth that Spirit simply Is - unknowable, unimaginable and indescribable. It may intellectually understand this, but the moment the mind searches for Reality it cannot contain it, as Pure Consciousness is beyond thoughts and ideas.

For something to be real - or the Absolute Truth - it by definition must be permanent. Reality cannot exist in one moment and cease to be in another moment, as it would then become false - Truth must exist eternally. As such, when the mind is directed outwards towards sensory phenomenon there is nothing in the entire cosmos that is unchanging – everything is vibrating and flowing in an unending stream of movement. Even when the mind is directed inwards towards the subjective personal world of thoughts and emotions, the same laws of impermanence apply, that is, all thoughts and emotions come and go. Nothing is found to be permanent or eternal in this dualistic paradigm. However, when the mind goes beyond thought and seeks its own source, what is ultimately found is the eternal Pure Consciousness witnessing itself through itself, as itself.

17

मानसं तु किं
मार्गणे कृते ॥
नैव मानसं
मार्ग आर्जवात् ॥१७॥

mānasaṃ tu kiṃ mārgaṇe kṛte
naiva mānasaṃ mārga ārjavāt

When an inquiry is made into what the mind actually is, one discovers that there is no such thing as mind. This is the direct path of yoga.

Jñāna Yoga is the inquiry into the origin of the mind. Because all other paths of *yoga* ultimately converge into the source of the mind, it is said that *Jñāna Yoga* is the direct means, whereas all other methods are indirect. The *karma yogi* who surrenders all action to the One, the *bhakti yogi* who worships the Beloved, or the *rāja yogi* who awakens *Shakti,* all reach the same destination. The One, the Beloved and *Shakti* are all different words that mean the same thing – the essential Source of Existence. Though these 3 grades of *yoga* all emphasize the same ultimate aim, their practices are indirect, using a means other than the goal.

Jñāna Yoga is unique in that its path is also its destination. That is, the principal techniques of *Jñāna Yoga,* which are centered on self- inquiry, directly reveal a state, which is beyond the mind. Through the spiritual technique of inquiry, or *vichāra,* the *jñāna yogi* has perpetual glimpses into the True Nature of Reality throughout their training. As Self-Awareness grows with inquiry Reality is directly intuited, and likewise as Self-Awareness diminishes, so too, does the view of Reality. Yet, through continual inquiry into the Self, these glimpses of Truth begin to become more vivid and longer lasting, until the vision of Reality becomes firmly established.

It may be said that *Jñāna Yoga* is considered to be the direct path to Self-Realization because it adheres strictly to the doctrine of non-duality, in comparison to all other paths of yoga. The *karma yogi* presupposes duality in the notion of a separate doer that is serving or surrendering their actions to another higher power. The *bhakti yogi* longs to be united with its Beloved, assuming separation between the two until final union. The raja yogi too, seeks to unite their individuality with the Supreme Consciousness as they initially assume an inherent division between the two. The *jñāna yogi* holds none of these illusions and seeks only to remove the ignorance, in the form of conceptual dualistic thought, from the ever present experience of Reality. Because of the inherent wisdom imbedded within non-dual teachings, the *jñāna yogi* not only senses the existence of the One Spirit, but through the practice of inquiry tastes it directly.

The experience which unfolds through inquiry into the Source, is like that of peeling away layer after layer of the conceptual mind until its very core is seen to be non-existent. The mind as such does not exist as a permanent entity in and of itself. It is merely a composition of layers of thought, ever changing and forming constructs and habitual patterns. As such, the mind, due to its impermanent nature, is said to be unreal or non-existent from the perspective of the Absolute.

18

वृत्त यस्त्वहं
वृत्ति माश्रिताः॥
वृत्त योमनो
विद्ध्य हंमनः॥१८॥

vṛttayastvahaṃ vṛttim-āshritāḥ
vṛttayo mano viddhyahaṃ manaḥ

All thoughts are dependent on the "I" thought. As such, know that the "I" thought is itself the primal thought.

Upon investigation into the nature of mind one discovers that there is in actuality no independent entity that can be identified as the mind. Mind is only a word that denotes the ever changing flow of thoughts moving through one's awareness. Trying to catch the mind is like trying to catch the wind – it is intangible and ungraspable. Mind does not really exist; in the same way that wind is nothing but air moving through space. As such, what we call mind is only thoughts, which in and of themselves are just as evasive as mind.

What are thoughts made of? Though the brain itself requires chemical substances to function the thoughts themselves have no physical substance. Thoughts, however, do have an origin. In order for thoughts to occur someone must be there to experience them. This thinker in each one of us we call "I." Each and every thought depends upon and originates in the "I" or individual ego. This egoic source of all thoughts is the root of the mind. As such, to go beyond thought and to experience the pure Bliss of Consciousness, we must inquire into the ego in the form of the "I" thought.

19

अहम यंकुतो
भवति चिन्वतः॥
अयिप तत्यहं
निजवि चारणम्॥१९॥

aham-ayaṃ kuto bhavati chinvataḥ
ayi patatyahaṃ nija-vichāraṇam

When searching for the source of the "I", it immediately vanishes through Self-inquiry.

The *Mahārshi* now reveals the principal method of *Jñāna Yoga* – Self-inquiry, or *ātma vichāra.* To search for the origin of the "I" thought is called Self-inquiry. This often takes the form of questioning oneself deeply though the inquiry "Who am I?" Or alternatively other lines of questioning such as, "From where does the "I" thought arise?" or "What is this I?" The central theme however remains the same. The emphasis is placed on isolating the feeling of "I," or "I am," or "I exist" and dwelling upon it.

This is not a mental exercise that demands a logical answer like "I am so and so...I was born here...my mother's name is this..." etc. It is only a tool to introvert the mind and rest it in the awareness of the ever-present experience of simply Being. The question can be repeated a few times over to draw the awareness inwards, as well, it may be beneficial to repeat the word "I" two or three times mentally afterwards.

This inquiry must be done with a calm and peaceful mind, which if necessary can be made so through any breathing technique that quiets the mind. This can be especially beneficial for times when there is a lot of mental and emotional restlessness or dullness of mind. The question must be intensely sincere with a strong determination to reveal the source of the "I" thought and one's own existence.

Upon this inquiry, when the mind is immersed in the inner search and close to the egoic "I," like an apparition, the "I" thought suddenly and immediately vanishes and a deep expanse of inner silence takes its place. At once, in only one moment, the very root of the ego is directly experienced as non-existent. Initially it may happen as a flash; so suddenly that one may not even be aware that the state beyond thought was actually experienced. With due practice, however, the momentary glimpses into Reality last longer and become more vivid before the normal flow of thinking resumes. This remarkably simple technique is similar to what some people call mindfulness, present moment awareness, living in the here and now, or awareness of the Higher Self. The uniqueness of Self-inquiry is that by using the seed thought "I" it becomes very easy and simple to access the Natural State directly with no other prop necessary.

20

अहमि नाशभा
ज्यहम हंतया ॥
स्फुरति हृत्स्वयं
परम पूर्णसत् ॥२०॥

ahami nāshabhājyaham-ahaṃtayā
sphurati ḥrt-svaya.m parama-pūrṇa-sat

Upon the egoic individual "I" being absorbed into the Heart, there emanates in its place the True Self, which is the Supreme and complete state of Being.

When through self-inquiry the feeling of an individual "I" disappears, in its place is experienced a radiant state of pure stillness. Many people experience an innate fear at the very idea of losing their individuality. This is natural but must be overcome by a proper understanding of what is actually being lost. For the experience of complete freedom, which is the ultimate goal of *yoga*, all limitations must be transcended. The self-limiting patterns of conceptualization held by the mind are the very form and root of bondage. These self-limiting patterns shape the very way we perceive the world, through the delusions of fear, jealousy, greed, anger, lust, pride and ignorance. How can you fully love when you hold on to fear? How can compassion express itself when one is self-obsessed with only one's own desires?

When all ideas, thoughts, and sentiments are let go of and Self-inquiry is followed intensely, the ego structure dissolves and what remains is the Natural State of complete spontaneity. No longer bound by the false projections of the ego trying to glorify itself, all pretensions, anxieties and selfishness is replaced by the essential and true Self. Inwardly peaceful, serene, full of innate wisdom, compassion and a repository of virtue, the Light of the Self expresses itself with no self-effort. In the loss of the ego it is not that the personality is lost, per se, but rather that Spirit is allowed to express itself fully through the enlightened mind.

Here the *Mahārshi* points out that this consummation takes place in the Sacred Heart. The Heart, called *hridayam,* is not to be confused with the physical heart or even the subtle *anāhata* heart *chakra*. The true Heart is Consciousness itself and is not limited to any location or center of the body. But because the confusion of identifying with the body/mind persists in the state of forgetfulness, and as a means to absorb the mind into the True Self, the *Mahārshi* makes a concession and would sometimes teach that this Sacred Heart originates in the chest, about two fingers width to the right of center. This instruction he expressed in some of his other works as being an effective tool for the unenlightened. But in Reality, he would say that the Heart is the all-pervading Consciousness, not bound to any location. However, as long as one is caught in the web of ignorance, forgetting the True Self, a spiritual seeker may focus their attention upon this Heart space in the center of the chest, while mentally inquiring "Who am I?"

21

इदम हंपदाऽ
भिख्य मन्वहम्॥
अहमि लीनके
प्यलय सत्तया॥२१॥

idam-ahaṃ-padābhikhyam-anvaham
ahami līnakepyalaya-sattayā

This True Self is that which always exists as Pure Being, even when the egoic "I" disappears; it never subsides.

To clarify what one is actually in search of, the *Mahārshi* suggests another common method of inquiry from *Jñāna Yoga*. *Avastha vichāra*, or inquiry into the three states of wakefulness, dreaming and deep sleep, illuminates the process of reclaiming Self-Awareness. It must be remembered that what is termed the egoic "I" is nothing but the mind which itself is only thoughts. By nature's design the mind is only capable of projecting itself upon Reality in the states of wakefulness and dreaming, but not in deep sleep.

If one reflects upon the nature of one's own experience of the deep sleep state, beyond dreams, it will become evident that each and every night the mind and personality cease to express themselves. In deep sleep no thought occurs and hence no personality manifests, yet the feeling of witnessing persists, with the True Self acting as the witness. There are no diverse or personal experiences that occur; as deep sleep is one continuous void-like expanse. In the deep sleep state even the concepts of time and space do not exist, as we are unable to recall for how long we've slept, where we were, and what boundaries existed to contextualize the experience.

It is this same witness, devoid of thoughts, that exists as the state of pure Being in all the three states of waking, dreaming, and deep sleep, and is called the Supreme Witness or the True Self. That very same witness is what persists in the waking and dreaming state even while thoughts occur. In these two states thoughts are projected upon the witnessing consciousness and identification with thoughts occur, whereas in deep sleep there are no thoughts to project, and hence the True Self is directly experienced. *Jñāna yogis* seek to become aware of this witnessing consciousness and recall its presence in all three states.

The deep sleep state is very near to the experience of enlightenment yet though we all experience it every night it is not experienced with awareness. We enter the deep sleep state due to lethargy and inertia and hence blank out during the experience. We recall only a vague, blank, darkness. Yogis however experience all three states with clarity and lucidity. When in deep sleep, yogis not only experience it as a thought free dimension, but also as a luminous expanse of Pure Light. This is a key distinction between one identified with the "I" thought and the ego, and the detached, egoless mind of an enlightened sage.

22

विग्र हेन्द्रिय
प्राण धी तमः॥
नाह मेकस
तज्ज डंह्यसत्॥२२॥

vigrahendriya-prāṇa-dhī-tamaḥ
nāham-eka-sat-taj-jaḍaṃ hyasat

The body, senses, vital force, intellect and ignorance are not the One Being, as they are unconscious and ultimately non-existent.

Another common technique of *Jñāna Yoga* to induce the clarity of vision necessary for Self-Awareness to dawn, is called neti-neti, or the method of cancelation. When we don't know what something is we can choose to negate what it is not, in order to eliminate all other possibilities. This is similar to being asked to find a diamond in a treasure chest of precious gems even though you have never seen a diamond before. By removing the gems you do know: the emeralds, rubies, sapphires, pearls and so on, what remains must be the diamond. By understanding clearly all that we are not, what is left is what we truly are.

This method of negation may seem strange at first as most people prefer to affirm the positive. Yet its brilliance lies in the simple truth that you are already the True Self, whether you are aware of it or not. As such the Self is nothing to be attained or gained. By your very nature, you are That. In order to realize this, all that needs to be done is to remove all the false concepts that obscure this recognition. In order to remember who you truly are you must forget all that you are not. As you already are the Self there is actually no need to proclaim it. The Self has always been your true nature, and will always be. Affirming that you are the Self, is as ridiculous as a woman saying to herself over and over again "I am a woman, I am a woman, I am a woman."

Jñāna yogis prefer to conclusively adopt the theoretical standpoint that they are already the complete spiritual Consciousness; always One and never having become dual. Yet in terms of certain stages of practice they must use reverse psychology, as it were, to dispel the ignorance of this fundamental truth by negating all that they are not. The Self is like the pure space in a room full of clutter. If you want to reveal the space in that room all that you need to do is remove all the clutter so that the pure space may be seen. In the same way, by simply removing the concepts that fill up the pure space of Consciousness, the True Self can be clearly seen.

This verse uses this particular methodology and states that neither the body, senses, *prāna*, intellect and the blank ignorance of sleep are the True Self. All of these phenomena are temporary, impermanent, and cannot exist apart from the witnessing agent – the True Self. None of these phenomena can function or be experienced without a seer or knower, which is the Witness Consciousness. As such they are said to be unconscious in and of themselves, as they require the True Self to enliven them.

23

सत्त्व भासिका
चित्क्व वेतरा ॥
सत्त याहि चि
चित्त याह्यहम्॥२३॥

sattva-bhāsikā chit-kva-vetarā
sattayā hi chich-chittayā hyaham

There cannot be another Consciousness to experience what Is. What Is, is the One Consciousness, and that itself is the True Self.

This verse is very subtle in its meaning and can be difficult to grasp unless the primary themes of Consciousness, What Is and the True Self are understood in their native Sanskrit context. In essence this statement is saying that all which is experienced, "That which Is", is itself Consciousness and the True Self. They are essentially synonyms that imply the same One state of Self-Awareness. Consciousness is called *chit* in Sanskrit and simultaneously conveys the idea of awareness and that which knows or experiences. Existence, Being, or That which Is, are all expressed by the word *sat*. The term *aham* denotes the True Self or witnessing agent.

What is being said in this verse is actually quite simple. Succinctly put, it is saying that everything experienced is Consciousness itself. Without consciousness nothing can be experienced and hence all that is experienced is made up of Consciousness. At the same time, it is Consciousness who is the witness of that which is being experienced; it is both the witness and the experience itself. There is no other entity other than the One Consciousness. It is the one who experiences, it is the act of experiencing, and it is the experience itself. As such Consciousness is itself the One Self and all that is experienced is that very same Self. Conscious is aware of itself as itself.

In the same way that the dream experience is a projection within the dreamer, so too is the waking experience a projection within the conscious wakeful state. The only distinction between the two is that during the dream state our outer senses are no longer functioning; that is, there are no physical sounds, sensations, sights, tastes or smells experienced. Instead, the inner senses apprehend the dream sensations and experience them as tangibly real. In the waking state the same sub-conscious thought-forms are projected upon our True Self, creating what appears to be reality. However, once the projection of thoughts have ceased, the appearance of the world also ceases; just as in the dream state, once one wakens from the dream and the mental projections have ceased, the dream too ceases.

It is like being in a dark movie theater watching images projected upon a screen, we get so immersed and attached to these images that we feel the story to be real. In the same way, we get so attached and connected with our thoughts and perceived experience, that we too, feel them to be real. Just as when the movie is over and the lights are turned on to reveal that what we experienced were only images being projected on a screen, one day, we too, will experience that what we perceive as reality is but a mere projection of thoughts upon Consciousness. All conscious, subconscious and unconscious thoughts are being projected upon the screen of Consciousness. To become aware of Consciousness as the substratum upon which all experience takes place, is referred to as the super-conscious state, known as the 4th state or dimension, called *turiya* in Sanskrit. In this enlightened state all is experienced as Consciousness, by Consciousness, and within Consciousness. The experiencer, the experiences and the act of experiencing all reveal themselves to be the One. Enlightenment is like waking up from a long dream of a life filled with imagined pleasure and pain – and that is why it is called Awakening.

24

ईश जीवयो
र्वेष धीभिदा ॥
सत्स्व भावतो
वस्तु केवलम् ॥२४॥

īsha-jīvayor-veṣa-dhī-bhidā
sat-svabhāvato vastu kevalam

In their true essence, God and the individual are the same One Being, they only differ in the scope of their form and capacity to know.

To understand the concept of a personal God as held by the sages, it is helpful to look at the meaning behind its Sanskrit name, *Īshwara. Īshwara* is composed of 3 unique syllables: *Īsha* + *Sva* + *Ra*. *Īsha* means perception, *sva* implies one's own innate nature and *ra* is the seed sound of the fire element, which denotes fire's innate luminosity. As such *Īshwara,* or God, is the perception of one's essential luminosity. This is why saints, sages and mystics throughout the world describe God in terms of Light- for that is God's essence. The *Mahārshi* goes one step further and asserts that this Light too is the essence of the individual. As such, in *yoga* philosophy, God and each individual are One.

The only distinction between God and individuals lies in their body and mind. So long as the egoic individuality endures, each creature's experience will be limited and localized to its particular body, be it human, cow, dog, tree, vegetable or even mineral.

The body of God contains the entirety of all individual beings, all of creation and is called Existence - which is unlimited, omnipotent and omniscient, capable of knowing all simultaneously. Whereas the mind of each individual's perception is limited to their particular level of mental and emotional evolution and its corresponding range of experience. And whereas the individual's range of influence is limited to the particular place they dwell for the duration of their lifespan, God is omnipresent, beyond the scope of time and space, and exists everywhere at all times.

Yet the *Mahārshi* points out that the essence of God and the individual is One. The same light of Consciousness that is within God is within the Heart of each individual. Once through self-inquiry, or any other method, the individual ego is dissolved into the Cosmic Whole, God is found to be everywhere and exists as everything. The individual becomes one with God.

25

वेष हानतः
स्वात्म दर्शनम्॥
ईश दर्शनं
स्वात्म रूपतः॥२५॥

veṣa-hāntaḥ svātma-darshanam
īsha-darshnaṃ svātma-rūpataḥ

Once the self-limiting factors of ignorance are removed, the vision of God in the form of one's own True Self emerges.

The self-limiting factors that veil our True Self are the habitual tendencies to identify with the body and mind. If we are able to divert our attention away from the senses and our tendencies towards attachment and aversion, and place our sole attention upon the Heart, at once the Presence of God is experienced. God is not unreachable or inaccessible to us in some far away heavenly realm. What is called God is nothing but Consciousness itself. Each one of us is intuitively aware of God or this Presence to a lesser or greater degree.

Though we often keep our awareness focused on the objects of our outer world or the objects of our inner world, such as thoughts, emotions, memories, or fantasies, we are rarely aware of Pure Consciousness itself. It is in those moments when we are able to perceive Reality as it is, without projecting our thoughts or emotions upon it, that the boundaries of the body and mind disappear - and what is left is Pure Awareness. In the purity of present moment awareness we transcend time and space, and touch the infinite, eternal Oneness. This paradoxically formless form is what people call God, without the awareness of what God truly is. It is only in the vast, silent, luminous expanse of allowing oneself to simply Be, that God can be known. God can only exist right here and now.

26

आत्म संस्थितिः
स्वात्म दर्शनम् ॥
आत्म निर्द्वया
दात्म निष्ठता ॥२६॥

ātma-saṃsthitiḥ svātma-darshanam

ātma-nirdvayād-ātma-niṣṭhatā

To be oneself is alone to know oneself, because who else can know the Self.

Because you are the One Consciousness, free of all duality, who can know you apart from yourself. The triad of knower, known and knowing all break down in the light of Self-Awareness. The only way to know your Self is to simply be your Self. In the simplicity of allowing yourself to Be, moment after moment, after moment, with no other concerns, you exist in your Natural State. This is the great revelation of *Jñāna Yoga*.

Even the term Self-Realization is misleading as there is nothing to be realized. To Be as you are in each and every moment is the highest form of spiritual practice. Nothing else needs to be done. Once the Natural State has been recognized, one needs to simply abide in it. This is what is actually meant by Self-Realization or knowing the Self. Simply let everything be as it is.

27

ज्ञान वर्जिताऽ
ज्ञान हीनचित् ॥
ज्ञान मस्ति किं
ज्ञातु मंतरम् ॥२७॥

jñāna-varjitā jñāna-hīna-chit
jñānam-asti kiṃ jñātum-antaram

Awareness that is free from objectivity is devoid of ignorance and is true knowledge. Apart from this, there is nothing else to be known.

This verse echoes another beautiful *Jñāna Yoga* aphorism found in the *Upanishads*. In this aphorism, a loving student asks their compassionate teacher "O glorious one please teach me that one thing, that by knowing which, all other things are known." Upon which the master skillfully and graciously replies "O best of students, yours whose heart is wide and mind made calm by the peace of meditation, by knowing that One, all other things are known!" That One thing is Consciousness itself, which is free from any conceptual knowledge.

The knowledge of the relative world is temporary, as all the objects within it are ever changing. Though useful for the practical purposes of living day-to-day life, the relative world does not offer the lasting peace, joy and happiness that we all seek. So long as one's awareness is projected outwards to know the objective phenomena of the world, the true knowledge of how to be completely free from suffering cannot dawn.

When instead, the mind is allowed to look within through self-inquiry, even the subjective knowledge of the egoic psyche dissolves. As one surrenders into the stillness of the Heart, the mist of ignorance which clouds the True Self, disperses to reveal the radiant nature of Reality. Once one witnesses Pure Consciousness through the direct experience of simply Being, there is nothing else to know. All that is worth knowing in order to experience eternal happiness has become known.

28

किंस्व रूपमि
त्यात्म दर्शने ॥
अव्य याऽभवा
पूर्ण चित्सुखम्॥२८॥

kiṃ svarūpam-ityātma-darshane
avyayābhavāpūrṇa-chit-sukham

Even a glimpse of the True nature of the Self fills one with the natural joy of Consciousness, which is all-pervading, unborn and inexhaustible.

Spiritual Consciousness is impossible to describe in words, yet the most succinct way that sages can describe it is as *sat-chit-ānanda*. *Sat* means Truth, existence or Being, *chit* means Awareness or Consciousness and *ānanda* means natural joy or bliss. These are not attributes of Spirit, but are what actually comprise it. Unless one has experienced the True Self, it is very difficult to grasp its indescribable nature. Yet what can be said is that it is a state in which one is blissfully enjoying being aware of their own existence. Self-Awareness, in its very nature is full of bliss. Inherently it has within it an inner joy that is not dependent upon anything outside of itself. As such, true happiness requires nothing but Self-Awareness for its existence. This natural bliss can be induced the very moment one wishes to focus on the natural state of Being, without doing anything else. Once touched upon, a sudden wave of inner happiness arises from the Heart and continues to exponentially increase the longer one maintains an awareness of it. Upon familiarity with this natural state, this inborn happiness continues to exist indefinitely. Happiness is inexhaustible as it depends only upon the awareness of the Self. It is the innate nature of Reality - that thoroughly enjoys witnessing its own existence. As such, the happiness that each one of us searches for is not to be found anywhere else but in the Heart. One need not seek to gain happiness, as happiness is our very nature. Becoming aware of this is called the path of *yoga*.

29

बन्ध मुक्त्यती
तं परं सुखम् ॥
विन्दतीह जी
वस्तु दैविकः ॥२९॥

bandha-muktyatītaṃ paraṃ sukham
vindatīha jīvas-tu daivikaḥ

When one thus realizes their inherent Divinity in the here and now, one experiences the Bliss that is beyond both bondage and liberation.

In the Bliss of Self-Awareness all duality dissolves. The extremes of bondage and liberation are discovered to be mere ideas – words with no real substance. Suffering is seen to be only the construct of an impure mind. Although both pain and pleasure are experienced even by the wise, it cannot disturb their eternal peace and Blissful Self-Awareness, as they are without attachment or aversion. Even the desire for liberation does not arise in the purity of non-conceptual wisdom. In the final phases of Self-realization even the desire for liberation is an obstacle on the path. That is, all conceptual thinking must eventually be dropped. It is only when one surrenders to what Is, abiding in the middle ground that transcends all opposites, can the Truth be revealed.

Once the ideas of bondage and liberation can be seen as mere constructs of the mind, the world no longer appears to be full of suffering, pain and dissatisfaction. Conceptual thinking is the greatest barrier to total freedom, and association with awakened sages is often required to attain this freedom. Compassion spontaneously emanates from the Hearts of illumined sages, and all who take shelter under their care and guidance soon realize their own Divinity. Such sages are as rare to find as the proverbial needle in the haystack. To keep their company is the pure benediction of Divine Grace, for it is they who show the way to Freedom.

30

अहम पेतकं
निजवि भानकम्॥
महदि दंतपो
रमण वागियम्॥३०॥

aham-apetakaṃ nija-vibhānakam
mahad-idaṃ tapo ramaṇa-vāgiyam

Abiding as the True Self, shining free of the ego is the only real spiritual practice. Thus says Ramana.

To remain in the non-conceptual Bliss of Self-Awareness is the quintessence of all spiritual practices. In truth it is the only effort that need be made. All other spiritual techniques are to control and focus the mind upon the Heart. Upon reaching this destination all that is left to do is to enjoy and dwell in the Heart for all of eternity. This is what is really meant by following the spiritual path. All other efforts are directed at simply finding the path. Once found, all that remains is to abide in it; for truly "the path is the destination." Keeping the mind free from thought in the luminous Heart is at the same time the path and the destination - Freedom - itself. Having taken us to the summit of spirituality, Ramana's final words of wisdom are simply to stay here. Simply be as you are – this is *yoga*.

Synopsis

Upadesha Sāram is a profound scripture that works on many levels simultaneously, allowing each to absorb whatever they are capable of. For some it appears that the four paths of *yoga* described are unique and independent practices that in and of themselves offer a complete pathway to the Absolute Consciousness. In this way, each path is conducive to suit the various temperaments of each spiritual seeker enabling them to attain liberation from the methods and means that suit them best.

Others, intuit that the four pathways of *yoga* can be viewed as natural extensions of each another, one leading to the other, like four steps of a ladder leading to the Supreme Goal. The self-less actions of the *karma yogi*, which are dedicated to the Supreme, naturally open one's Heart. Once the Heart is open, the natural yearning to express love, gratitude and devotion of the *bhakti yogi* emerges. Through this intense focalization of all thoughts and emotions upon the Beloved, the single-pointed meditation of the *rāja yogi* develops and further purifies the mind. Finally, with a still and focused mind concentrated at the Heart, the innate wisdom of the *jñāna yogi* dawns and pursues Self-Inquiry, waiting for the True Nature of Self to be revealed. Once this glimpse of Reality has been experienced, all that is left to do is abide in its formless Presence.

Others may see these four paths of yoga in the paradoxical manner that the *Mahārshi* also brilliantly expounds. That is, in Reality the four paths of *yoga* do not really exist. There is only one spiritual path, that of the Heart, where all pathways eventually culminate. This is similar to an ascent up to the top of a very steep mountain. Along the ascent there are many trails, but once one nears the top, all paths must converge into one.

Ultimately when the top of the summit is reached, with the feet having nowhere else to go, one stands upon a pathless path. It is only from the top of the mountain that one can have the vast and equal vision of everything below. The same One True Self enlivens the waking, dreaming, sleeping and *samadhi* states. Once known, through the complete stillness of mind in each and every moment, it itself reveals the pathless path and resolves all doubts.

In the *Mahārshi's* own words: "Whatever means one may choose, the "I" is inescapable, the "I" that does the selfless service, the "I" that yearns for joining the Lord from whom it feels it has been separated, the "I" that feels it has forgotten its real nature, and so on. The source of this "I" must be found out. Then all questions will be answered."

OM TAT SAT

श्री

उपदेशसारः॥

संपूर्णः॥

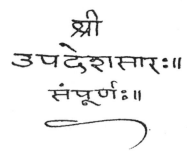

Appendix

Complete text of the

Upadesha Sāram

in free flowing English

1. Through the inherent order of Nature actions give results. Is Karma then Absolute? No, it is constantly changing and lacks Consciousness.
2. Activity is obstructive to liberation, as any results obtained are impermanent, thus creating more bondage.
3. Actions done while remembering the One and without a desire for their intended results, purify the mind and are a means towards liberation.
4. The actions done through body, speech and mind, such as rituals, chanting and meditation, are increasingly superior in this ascending order.
5. Selfless service done, while holding the view that the world is itself Spirit, is the true worship of the One in all its forms.
6. Better than singing songs in praise of Spirit, is the repetition of sacred sounds, either aloud, by whisper or mentally.
7. Unbroken attention, which flows smoothly like the water of a river, is superior to focus which waivers.
8. Meditating with the attitude that "I am Spirit" is more purifying than meditation which posits a separation between the individual and the Supreme.
9. By the strength of this type of meditation, one becomes established in the state of True Being, devoid of all thoughts, which is the Supreme Devotion.
10. Resting the mind in its natural state within the sacred space of the Heart is the essence of karma, bhakti, raja and jnana yoga.

11. By restraining the breath the mind becomes still like a bird caught in a net. This is an efficient method to control the mind.

12. The mind, which has the function of knowing and the vital air with the function of doing, are like two branches of the One Cosmic Energy that is the Source.

13. Restraint of mind is of two types; dissolution by which the mind subsides temporarily but later resumes functioning, and dissolution by which complete stillness is attained without the mind ever reemerging.

14. The mind, having subsided by restraining the breath, becomes permanently still by intensely focusing on a singular thought.

15. There is nothing left to do for the yogi who has conquered the mind and is established forever in the Natural State of Being.

16. Setting aside the fascination with both the objective and subjective phenomenon, when the mind looks within to find itself, all that is seen is Consciousness – the One Reality.

17. When an inquiry is made into what the mind actually is, one discovers that there is no such thing as mind. This is the direct path of yoga.

18. All thoughts are dependent on the "I" thought. As such, know that the "I" thought is itself the primal thought.

19. When searching for the source of the "I" it immediately vanishes through Self-inquiry.

20. Upon the egoic individual "I" being absorbed into the Heart, there emanates in its place the True Self, which is the Supreme and complete state of Being.

21. This True Self is that which always exists as Pure Being, even when the egoic "I" disappears; it never subsides.

22. The body, senses, vital force, intellect and ignorance are not the One Being, as they are unconscious and ultimately non-existent.

23. There cannot be another Consciousness to experience what Is. What Is, is the One Consciousness, and that itself is the True Self.

24. In their true essence God and the individual are the same One Being, they only differ in the scope of their form and capacity to know.

25. Once the self-limiting factors of ignorance are removed, the vision of God in the form of one's own True Self emerges.

26. To be oneself is alone to know oneself, because who else can know the Self.

27. Awareness that is free from objectivity is devoid of ignorance and is true knowledge. Apart from this, there is nothing else to be known.

28. Even a glimpse of the True nature of the Self fills one with the natural joy of Consciousness, which is all-pervading, unborn and inexhaustible.

29. When one thus realizes their inherent Divinity in the here and now, one experiences the Bliss that is beyond both bondage and liberation.

30. Abiding as the True Self, shining free of the ego is the only real spiritual practice. Thus says Ramana.

For more information
on the teachings of
Shri Ramana Mahārshi
please visit

www.sriramanamaharshi.org

and for more information on
Rāmānanda's teaching schedule
please visit

www.blooming-lotus-yoga.com